684
THO

Thorlin, Anders

Ideas for
woodturning

DATE			
NOV 19 '81			
DEC 4 '81			
NOV 16 '82			

Ideas for Woodturning

Anders Thorlin lives and works in Sweden. Surrounded by the natural material that he loves, he has developed an individual philosophy and approach to woodturning.

The Art & Design Series

For beginners, students, and working professionals in both fine and commercial arts, these books offer practical, how-to introductions to a variety of areas in contemporary art and design.

Each illustrated volume is written by a working artist, a specialist in his or her field, and each concentrates on an individual area—from advertising layout or printmaking to interior design, painting, and cartooning, among others. Each contains information artists will find useful in the studio, in the classroom, and in the marketplace.

Books in the Art & Design Series

Ideas for Woodturning

Anders Thorlin

A SPECTRUM BOOK

PRENTICE-HALL, INC., Englewood Cliffs, N.J. 07632

Library of Congress Cataloging in Publication Data

Thorlin, Anders.
  Ideas for woodturning.

  (A Spectrum Book)
  Translation of Ideer for Trasvarving.
  Bibliography: p. 107
  Includes index.
    1. Turning.   I. Title.
TT201.T4813 1980   684'.083   80-16562
ISBN 0-13-450361-9
ISBN 0-13-450353-8 (pbk.)

A SPECTRUM BOOK

10 9 8 7 6 5 4 3 2 1

Printed in the United States of America

Editorial/production supervision by Frank Moorman
Cover design by Tony Ferrara Studio, Inc.
Manufacturing buyer: Barbara A. Frick

PRENTICE-HALL INTERNATIONAL, Inc., *London*
PRENTICE-HALL OF AUSTRALIA PTY. LIMITED, *Sydney*
PRENTICE-HALL OF CANADA, LTD., *Toronto*
PRENTICE-HALL OF INDIA PRIVATE LIMITED, *New Delhi*
PRENTICE-HALL OF JAPAN, INC., *Tokyo*
PRENTICE-HALL OF SOUTHEAST ASIA PTE. LTD., *Singapore*
WHITEHALL BOOKS LIMITED, *Wellington, New Zealand*

Contents

Ideas for Woodturning

Introduction

Trees have always had a strong imaginative pull. On the one hand they are objects of natural beauty, symbols of strength and endurance, and on the other they are continuously-growing, living things whose form alters with the seasons. To snap off a twig, to cut into the bark is to inflict an injury. Sad as it may seem when a tree, one which has, perhaps, stood in the same spot for centuries, is felled in minutes with a power saw, it is at least some consolation if the now inanimate timber is used to make lasting objects of beauty.

This book is principally intended as a source of suggestions for woodturning and I have presupposed some knowledge of the techniques involved. Naturally, I hope that it will also inspire readers who have never turned wood and encourage them to take up what is a very rewarding craft and one that is by no means as difficult as it looks. Listed in the bibliography on page 107 you will find reference to several books on turning which, combined if possible with one of the many courses advertised in woodworking magazines, will give the necessary grounding in the use of the tools and equipment to enable you to make items similar to those illustrated here.

It is my intention to show nature as a source of inspiration and, at the same time, to draw the reader's attention to the traditional shapes and patterns of turnery by giving examples of their adaptation to a wide selection of modern items. Whether the impetus is recreational or commercial, working in wood gives one a keen feeling for nature. Personally, I feel that a tree epitomizes Nature's beauty and inspires in me an unceasing curiosity; whether from examination of the outside or by looking at the inner structure one gains an insight into its cycle. In an age when people and nature are so ruthlessly separated, it is a revitalising experience to come into contact with natural materials and especially with wood.

In furnishing our homes we have long tried to create as homogeneous a setting as possible, particularly where wood is used. The presence of knots, discolouration and other imperfections has been and often is considered undesirable in panelled walls and furniture. It is as if there has been a concerted effort to reduce this living material to the predictability of artificial board instead of exploiting its individuality to achieve a varied and visually stimulating result. This book will show how it is possible to use a greater variety of imperfections than already mentioned, for instance to work with a whole tree trunk, with or without its bark, to incorporate branches, swellings and the surface changes wrought by disease – to exploit rot-damaged or insect-infested timber.

Important sources of ideas are the many well-made articles of old turnery which one can still come across in plenty: the banisters of an old house, the legs of old-fashioned chairs and tables, the carved wooden ornaments and furniture still to be found in many churches.

A tree which has taken a hundred years to grow can be felled with a power saw in minutes. If it had to be felled it is good to know that something beautiful can be made from it.

Think in terms of adapting, say, the design of a pillar to the scale of a lamp stand; try not to associate certain items with specific shapes. In this book there are examples where the same pattern of turning is repeated in a table, standard lamps, a spice rack, goblets, cork-screws and so forth; all that is different is the scale. Look at a turned item and imagine how it would be if it were enlarged or diminished, if only certain parts of the design were used or if other designs were combined. I hope that the reader will use the examples here in just such a way. Enlarged, half a cork-screw could become the base of a lamp or the the end of a curtain rod.

There are traditional turnery shapes which have been in use for hundreds of years; by different combinations of these designs you will achieve an originality which has developed from this tradition. I think highly of the old examples of turnery with their perfectly rounded forms, and their clear-cut markings which make the turning stand out and give a clean and neat appearance. That is not to say they should look 'complicated'; the plain, modern shape is often acknowledged as beautiful and can be more difficult to turn since there are no visible markings for guidance.

As the popularity of wooden articles continues, so the quantity of poor quality items increases and it becomes particularly important to convince people of the need to rediscover and preserve the old shapes and the craft that has produced them. We must appreciate the importance of Nature and learn to cherish, not squander the materials she provides.

There are a great many items, including the ones illustrated here, for which a turning lathe and perfectly simple machinery will be quite adequate. A little thought and an observant eye cast around your own home and surroundings should reveal any number of things which could be made of wood instead of plastic or any other synthetic material. Many of them are round, such as knobs for doors, drawers, cupboards, stoppers for bottles and jars – all of which could be turned from wood.

Inspired by nature

Trunk, bark and branches

As I mentioned earlier, the external form of a tree often provides an imaginative stimulus which should not be neglected. By preserving the trunk, by making use of the bark, branches and twigs, you greatly extend your creative possibilities. The bowl on top of the felled trees in the picture on the next page is an example of this type of work. Made from a sawn-off piece of pine trunk, it has a diameter of 270mm (10$\frac{5}{8}$in) and has been treated with a plastic coating. You may be lucky enough to come across similarly suitable pieces in the wild and you should follow the procedure underlined; if not, then this description will show you what is involved in preparing raw unseasoned timber for turning.

Freshly-felled timber may have a moisture content of eighty per cent or more compared with the open air where the atmosphere may be something like twenty per cent. The green log will, therefore, surrender its moisture to the air until its moisture content is in balance with that of the surrounding atmosphere, e.g. twenty per cent. When this balance is achieved the timber is said to be 'seasoned' for that particular moisture content. This process of drying out is accompanied by a loss of weight and volume and if it is done too quickly warping, splitting and other defects invariably result. The whole object of seasoning is to make the wood as stable as possible given the conditions to which it will finally be exposed.

The sort of timber from which the bowl was made, timber 'in the round', requires additional time to season since the thicker the timber the longer this takes. To speed

Consider the possibility when turning of retaining the bark or making use of branches and twigs.

The candle holder on the left is of birch, the one in the middle, with the bark, is of alder and the two small ones are of oak.

things up, it is best to reduce the log roughly to the anticipated size required *before* seasoning.

It is a common practice to rough turn thick timber which is wet, especially if one intends to use it for bowls, and then set it aside to dry off before finishing. It is, of course, necessary to leave such turnings very full in size, otherwise there will not be enough timber to turn the final shape.

16

Stored in a dry, airy place out of direct sunlight, these will be ready in two or three months. They will have warped and twisted but can be returned to the lathe for finishing.

Should you intend to do your own seasoning, remember that although timbers differ in their seasoning characteristics, a good rule is to allow twelve months air drying time for every 25mm (1in) of timber thickness. Paint the end grains of the timber with thick lead paint or paraffin wax and cross-pile the pieces off the ground on an open-air site so air can circulate round them for six months. Protect the top of the stack from the weather. Afterwards, cross-pile again in an airy, under-cover position for a further six months per 25mm (1in) of thickness. A final three months in a moderately warm room and your timber should be ready for use.

The candle holders illustrated on page 15 are from 120mm to 280mm (4¾in to 11in) high. The small ones are of oak, the one with the twig 'handle' is birch, and the largest with the bark still on is made of alder.

The candle holder on page 16 has two 'legs'. The log has been turned upside-down and the branches form the legs. The timber used was rot-damaged aspen, the finished height is 350mm (12in) and the holder was turned between

Left: the trunk has been turned upside-down and the branches make the two legs.

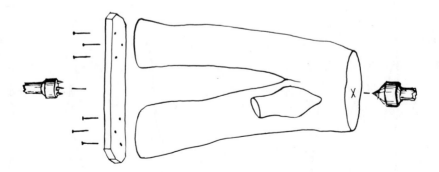

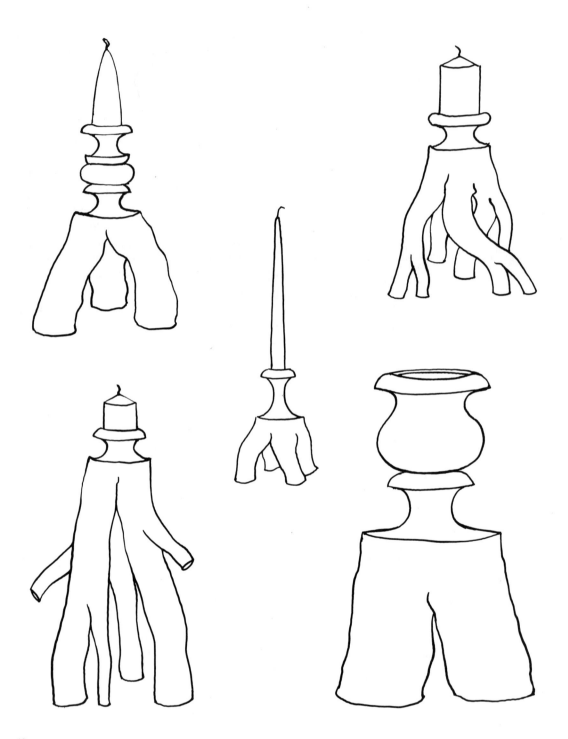

the lathe centres after a piece of deal had been temporarily attached as shown in the diagram. The other line drawings provide further ideas for incorporating branches into your project.

Worm-eaten material

It can be a rewarding experience to use timber which shows the markings and decay of nature's activity. Insect grubs, laid inside trees, gnaw intensely before they turn into pupae and again before their metamorphosis into butterflies or beetles. They live for a summer, perhaps laying new eggs, and then they die. Many of these insects have managed to destroy entire forests in a comparatively short time and are, therefore, regarded as pests. Yet their damage has an indisputable beauty of its own; their labours produce intricate passages, fascinating patterns in the wood. Since their life cycle and the damage it causes are part of nature, surely we should not dismiss them as mere pests?

The log and the candle holder on page 20 are of fir, a tree which is often infested with insects. Should you wish to make use of wood damaged in this way, ensure that the insects are gone by first treating it with some proprietary insecticide which does not stain the wood; it would be rather unpleasant to come across larvae while sawing or once turning had begun! When you have cut off a piece, carefully scrape off any remnants of bark and then remove 'sawdust' from the passages with a brush.

The candle holder illustrated on page 20 was turned on a screw chuck and care was taken to retain the small outgrowth. The piece is 130mm (5$\frac{1}{8}$in) and meant for a 12mm ($\frac{1}{2}$in) taper. The finished article was treated with a mixture of turpentine and raw linseed oil which gives lustre and penetrates deep into the wood. Any hapless grub which might have survived till then will surely perish under this onslaught!

Candle holders of juniper wood

Working with juniper wood is a particular pleasure because of the lovely scent it exhales. In most cases the wood is sawn according to requirements and treated like other timbers. The candle holders and lamp stand shown on pages 21 and 22 are a further instance of how the tree's external shape can be exploited. The irregularities

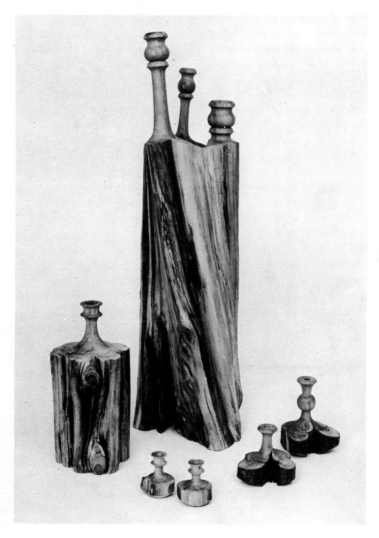

Left: the intricate patterns made by insects boring through the wood can be retained on your turning.

Right: the irregular growth of the juniper with its twists and .creases adds interest to these candle holders.

A trunk is often a sculpture in itself without any additional treatment. Here it has been made into a lamp stand.

inherent in the growth of the juniper, its twists and creases, are of special interest, for a trunk in its natural state may well have the appearance of a sculpture. The intriguing-looking tall candle holder on page 21 is made of a juniper trunk several centuries old. When I came across this log its heartwood was quite decayed. The log was first split into three and the largest and deepest creases exploited to the best possible advantage. Each part was then cut and turned separately. Finally, the three parts were glued together again. The holder measures 800mm ($31\frac{1}{2}$in) at its highest point. The smallest candlesticks are 70mm ($2\frac{3}{4}$in) high. The lamp stand on page 22 is 600mm ($23\frac{5}{8}$in) high.

An old apple tree

If you study the candle holders shown on page 36 you will see that inspiration for their design came from the inner, rot-damaged timber. By comparison, the lamp stand illustrated on page 25 and the candle holders on page 24 were inspired by external characteristics, the small outgrowths and knots of the old apple tree from which they were made. In order that these irregularities stand out, the bark should be removed and the knots brushed with a steel brush mounted on an electric drill. Once the bark has been removed, give your imagination free rein so that your cutting will show off the particular peculiarities of the piece. The candle holders, page 24, remind me of a group of people talking to each other. They are between 100mm (4in) and 150mm ($5\frac{7}{8}$in) high. The lamp stand, page 25, is 300mm ($11\frac{3}{4}$in) high.

24

Working with old timber

Demolition timber

It is often the case that pine made available by demolition work is of better quality than that sold by timber merchants. A particularly attractive wood, it can occasionally be purchased from demolition sites and its warm colours and 'olde-worlde' smell make it a joy to work.

In former times, when there was no shortage of wooded land, the craftsman could pick out the sort of timber he required with comparative ease. Nowadays, forestry is a serious and specialised business and timber resources are greatly diminished. However, the enterprising woodworker may come across beams from the seventeenth or eighteenth centuries with fresh-smelling heartwood still containing drops of resin. In my home country of Sweden many old wooden houses have been demolished and much fine timber burnt or disposed of by other means. Sadly, I have seen innumerable old buildings disappear in my own home town, but I profited from the event whenever possible by contacting the demolition workers and acquiring the old timber. The best material was to be found among the roof truss beams and, once this had been split up, I treated it like any other timber.

The candle holders and lantern, pages 28 and 29, show

that an entire block complete with cracks and nails may easily be used. Personally, I feel that these aspects add character and 'belong'. The old, often hand-forged nails would have to be removed before turning and then can be replaced in the finished article. Similarly, the cleaned and polished cracks enhance the decorative effect of the whole.

The selection of candle holders on pages 30 and 31, 100mm (4in) to 470mm (18½in) high, are made from blocks varying in size from 75mm × 75mm (3in square) to 203mm × 203mm (8in square). The lantern on the next page, with mouth-blown glass from Mantoprs Glasbruk, Sweden, stands 310mm (12¼in) high. The lamp stand on page 32 is made of a tarred block 152mm × 152mm (6in square) with a height of 470mm (18½in). After the final

Candle holders made from fir. The wood came from roof trusses and floor timbers of a demolished house.

polishing all the candle holders were treated with one part raw linseed oil to one part turpentine. For a really lustrous finish it is advisable to work this mixture in several times, allowing each individual layer to dry.

Candle holder from an old fir flooring block. The crackled glass lantern was mouth-blown.

Rot-damaged hardwood

Walking along lonely forest tracks you may chance upon stacks or single logs of hardwood, forgotten and discarded because of rot – not even considered good enough for firewood. Do not scorn them, for they offer a valuable source of material to the craftsman.

This lamp stand was made from a tarred fir block. The impregnation of the tar gives an effect rather like rot-damaged wood.

When once you begin to work with such wood you will discover how fantastic its patterning is and how varied its colouring. These unusual effects are a result of the combined activity of autumn downpours and the dry spells of summer. It is a process not unlike what happens when a pair of leather shoes get wet and dry off to leave white markings. You may have difficulty finding timber at

Candle holders made from rot-damaged rowan. This wood can reveal the most fantastic patterns and colours and there are many surprises as you work on it. Compare these with the illustrations on pages 34, 36 and 37.

just the right stage of decay: sufficiently rotten to have produced interesting changes in the wood but not so far advanced as to render it unusable. A log that has been lying on the ground is often so rotten that one cannot work it; the best material is usually to be found in the middle of a pile as those pieces will have been exposed to both damp and dryness most evenly. Remember, should

This lamp stand is made from rot-damaged birch which has developed a sort of growth caused by injury to the trunk some time ago.

38

you be lucky enough to find such timber, contact the owner or the appropriate body before removing your find.

The photographs of candle holders and lamp stands on pages 38 to 42 give examples of the use to which rot-damaged wood can be put, and the fact that one can

Left: Candle holder made from rot-damaged aspen to hold a handmade candle. The natural outline of the trunk has been cut away.

Right: candle holder also made from rot-damaged aspen to hold a hand-made, three-branched candle. Part of the trunk has been retained.

preserve the outline of the trunk gives these items a special value. The candle holders are made from rot-damaged aspen, birch and mountain ash (rowan). They are between 120mm ($4\frac{3}{4}$in) and 300mm ($11\frac{3}{4}$in) high and intended for candles with a diameter of between 12mm ($\frac{1}{2}$in) and 80mm ($3\frac{1}{8}$in). The small lamp, page 35, the stand of which has the same shape as the candle holders, is made of rot-damaged birch and is 150mm ($5\frac{7}{8}$in) high. The taller stand, page 40, has a height of 360mm ($14\frac{1}{8}$in) and is made of bubinga, which is an imported timber more commonly known as rosewood.

To make pieces similar to those described above you should, of course, first cut the log up into the required sections. Then remove any bark which may still be left and apply a wire or steel brush on an electric drill to remove the most tenuous of the porous wood. It is safest to put the block to be turned between centres and to work at as high a speed as possible without taking any risks. If the turning is done too slowly the finished surface will be uneven and there are likely to be great contrasts in the block between the hard and any porous timber. For a good finish much patient sandpapering is needed to ensure smoothness. The completed lamp stands and candle holders illustrated were treated several times with equal parts of raw linseed oil and turpentine. This treatment has the effect of making the different colours and patterns stand out more clearly; it also helps to bind such wood which is often very porous.

Rot-damaged wood is also well-suited to many other purposes which make good use of its particular qualities such as bowls, dishes and mats for bottles and sandwiches. Naturally, it is quite unnecessary to turn mats; it is simply a matter of cutting the block slantwise, rather like slicing bread, and then polishing it. The angle makes it more difficult for any knots in the piece simply to fall out.

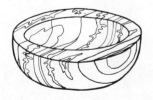

This lamp stand is turned throughout and made from bubinga or rosewood.

Illustrated on page 42 is an ornament in the form of a

41

small pendant mirror made of mountain ash which is suspended in one end of a hollow aspen block. The outside diameter of the pendant varies from 70mm ($2\frac{3}{4}$in) to 90mm ($3\frac{1}{2}$in) and that of the mirror glass is 40mm ($1\frac{5}{8}$in). This is made in the same way as the pendant mirror described on page 72 with the only difference being that the former still has the outline of the branch intact.

A small pendant mirror made from rot-damaged mountain ash. It is suspended in a hollow aspen trunk.

Experimenting with wood

The egg, an original shape

The egg, its shape and symbolism is an eternal source of fascination. Turning this particular shape, one is forced to consider not only the technique involved but also the texture required and the difficulties inherent in the particular form. The shape has beauty, the surface a satisfying smoothness; holding a well-turned egg in one's hand gives a special sense of fulfilment.

The display of beautiful turned eggs on pages 44 and 45 shows items made from different types of wood with heights varying from 30mm ($1\frac{1}{4}$in) to 150mm ($5\frac{7}{8}$in). Beginning with the eggs on stands, that on the extreme left is made of rot-damaged aspen, the next of pine, as is the second in from the extreme right. The largest egg was turned from a block of rotted rosewood and the one next to it, which looks as if it has been painted, has the startling patterns of rot-damaged mountain ash. The adjacent egg, marginally bigger, is made of laburnum and the one on the extreme right is of walnut. Working from the left again, the first three eggs lying down on the flat are of laburnum, the paler one lying directly in front of the very largest example is made from rot-damaged aspen, the small, mottled egg and the one on the extreme right are both of cross-grained birch and the two in

44

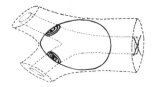

between are further examples from laburnum. The larger of the two eggs which face forward reminds me rather of a small wide-eyed animal: a marmot, perhaps. The 'eyes' are in fact obtained by turning a piece from which two twigs branched out. The diagram on this page explains this point.

At this juncture it might be worth while providing a bit of information for those who wish to produce animal-like toys. When making the little marmot, the position of the branching-out of the twigs was used in such a way as to give the impression that the 'head' is in the middle of the parting. Sometimes one can exploit twigs to form a mouth, a nose, ears or some other realistic feature. Obviously, the turned animal form does not have to originate from an egg shape, but for those that do the egg can be turned either at the mandrel for bowl turning or between centres. A good rub with oil will enhance the colour, pattern and smoothness of the piece.

Bear in mind that the turning of eggs can be done in a number of ways. With particular reference to those shown here on stands, the simplest method is to prepare your block of wood to size and mount it on a woodscrew chuck which allows you to turn both egg and base without having to re-chuck. A good look at the examples shows that the best and visually most interesting grain effects can be achieved only if one spares a little time before any cutting is done to consider how the grain runs. One of the most satisfying aspects of woodturning is to be able to utilise even the small, otherwise useless offcuts of timber and to exploit their grain and figure to the best possible advantage. With reference to the smaller eggs, an alternative method would be to turn them between centres in short lengths of two or three eggs, subsequently parting them off with a saw or finishing the ends by hand.

Hangings

An interesting and practical way of using a variety of turned shapes would be to suspend them as a form of curtaining to partition off part of a room. The curtain illustrated came into being in an impromptu manner. Occasionally, one turns items which are not good enough

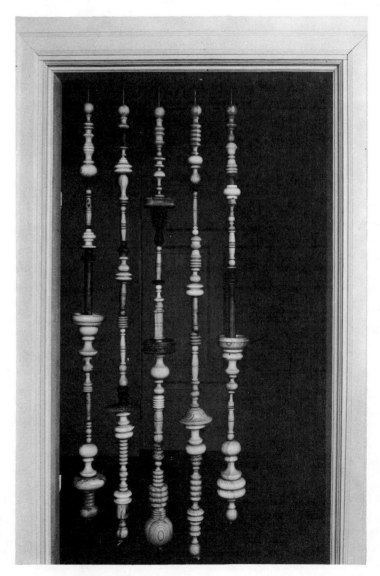

Curtain assembled from a variety of turned shapes. Among the many different woods used are fir, juniper, walnut, teak and oak.

for their original purpose or are so far from what was intended that in a fit of frustrated temper one tends to throw them out. A less wasteful and more positive way of using such items would be to finish the job of turning and then put the piece into a special box in which a collection of such oddments can be made; however good a turner you are, the box should not take too long to fill! This way and with the minimum of trouble you acquire a varied selection; by arranging them as you please you will be able to judge whether there is sufficient variety and length for the design you intend and, if not, you can turn more of the particular type you feel to be lacking. The only thing left is to drill holes through every piece and thread them on to leather thongs or nylon cord; ordinary string will usually come untwined and often is not strong enough.

For the playground

Many people find toys and play equipment both more acceptable and more beautiful when they are made from wood and this offers an ideal sphere for the use of turning techniques. The swing in the picture on page 49 is made of birch. If you examine the diagram you will see that it has been turned in two parts; the seat is made from one piece of timber 50mm (2in) thick and 300mm (11¾in) in diameter. The upper part is 220mm (8¾in) long without the pin and 80mm (3⅛in) wide at its broadest. Should it prove necessary to glue several pieces together for the seat to be big enough, it is best to use a waterproof adhesive. A few words of caution on the turning of timber which has been glued: always allow the glued blocks twenty-four hours in a warm room to cure the glue and ensure that it is set. When turning, *never* run the lathe too fast; take light cuts and keep your tools sharpened. It is also sound policy never to stand in direct line when doing any faceplate work in case the piece or a section disintegrates and fragments or chips fly at you, a particular danger where the work is a glued-up assembly. Wearing goggles is a further advisable safety precaution.

The whole swing is coated with marine varnish to cope with outdoor conditions. It has one through-going hole

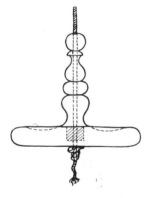

The swing in action.

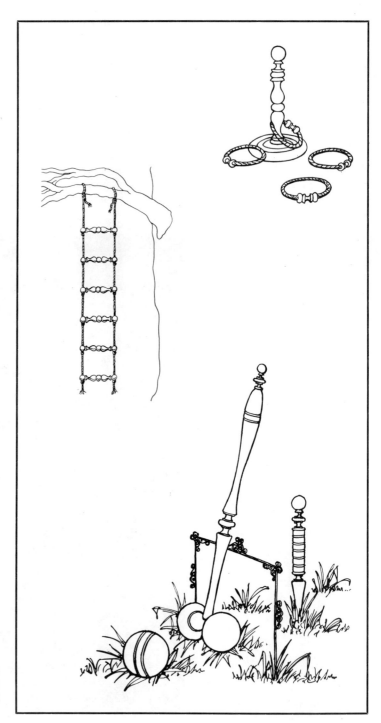

The somewhat old-fashioned design suits this croquet set. The mallet head should be turned in a strong wood such as cross-grained birch.

to take what must be very strong rope, here 12mm ($\frac{1}{2}$in) thick nylon, and the swing can then be suspended in a way that ensures free rotation. I must warn against making the swing too heavy; it would be quite dangerous if a small child were to collide with it and could cause nasty head injuries. With adult supervision or for the slightly older child the swing is a truly delightful piece of play equipment.

In addition here are some general suggestions for other turned play items: a ladder, croquet equipment, both mallet and ball, and quoits. When turning the rungs for the ladder bear in mind that they should be ridged in such a way as to provide a good grip for climbing; if you study the diagram you will see that stability is maintained by resting each rung on knots in the rope. When making the croquet equipment remember to turn the mallet in a strong wood like cross-gained birch or a root timber so that it will not shatter under the continued force of the blows. The ball is a straightforward piece of turning. With regard to the quoits illustrated in the diagram, the catching pins should be turned in the same way as the paper-roll holders described on page 90. The rings are made of pieces of rope glued together in the bore of a turned knob.

Wooden utensils

Bowls and dishes

Here are some examples of fruit bowls, salad bowls, bread-trays, serving trays and plates. A feature common to them all is that each is turned from a whole piece of wood. A bowl made from a glued-up assembly can never

Fruit or salad bowls turned from birch.

These plates were turned from a thick birch plank.

Bread trays made from demolition timber. The one on the table is made from spruce and the one standing is fir.

give the same feeling as that made from a single piece but very large bowls can often be made in no other way. Sizeable pieces of wood are particularly interesting to work since there is a large enough area to see the grain in its entirety.

The fruit or salad bowls shown on page 52 have a diameter of 300mm (11¾in) and are made from a thick, old birch board. Age gives them a somewhat dark and warm colouring. The plates or porridge bowls illustrated on page 53 are of the same material, the small ones are 210mm (8¼in) in diameter and the large one 270mm (10⅝in). The bread plate shown on page 53 has a diameter of 400mm (15¾in). The one lying on the table is made of spruce and the upright one is made from an old fir board, both blanks originating from demolition sites. The bowls and dishes can be turned on a 64mm (2½in) woodscrew chuck which is excellent for work up to 200mm (7¼in) to 225mm (8¼in) diameter but above this it is preferable to use a faceplate.

It should be remembered that wood is not the perfect medium for bowls, plates or goblets and that common-sense is required in caring for the finish. These bowls and plates should be treated with several coats of polyurethane or one of the specially prepared oil finishes. The latter should always be applied sparingly and worked well into the wood; several light coats should be applied allowing a day or two between each for hardening. Olive oil is useful for cleaning the insides and will keep the varnish film in good shape. It will also impart an appropriate aroma to your salad bowls! Should thorough cleaning be necessary, use a wash leather with the minimum of soap, rinsing under a cool tap and finally drying with a cloth.

When hollowing out be sure not to let your concentration wander, measure the thickness occasionally otherwise there is a real danger of letting the sides become so thin that they break.

Cutting boards

These are useful items not only for cutting and chopping but also for serving and as stands for hot dishes. The cutting boards shown below are made of old oak, which was originally part of a staircase in a now-demolished building, and of birch. Both these timbers resist damp well. The boards are between 40mm (1½in) and 50mm (2in) thick, 170mm (6¾in) to 250mm (9¾in) wide, and 300mm (11¾in) and 450mm (17¾in) long. The round board has a diameter of 350mm (13¾in) and has been turned on a screw chuck (you may find a faceplate easier). To finish off, olive oil or one of the proprietary oils which are on sale should be worked in, the piece cleaned with a damp cloth and a further, sparing coat of oil applied. Proprietary finishes will leave neither taste nor smell. Remember, just as with all other wooden household utensils, these boards will usually warp after they have been washed up and dried with a damp cloth several times. Obviously, it is then necessary to renew the oil rub.

These cutting boards are made from old stair boards with turned handles. The woods used, oak and birch are resistant to damp.

Butter knives made from juniper wood which is especially suitable for the purpose.

56

Butter knives

The butter knives in the photograph on page 56 are made of juniper, a wood specially suited for the purpose. Besides having that wonderful scent, the wood is pliant and it is possible to carve very thin and flexible blades. If you are careful with the knife in early use, it tends to become more pliable for spreading in accordance with the butter being worked into the wood. Those shown are between 150mm ($5\frac{7}{8}$in) and 200mm ($7\frac{7}{8}$in) long. The handle has been turned as shown in the diagram, page 56, and then the blade carved with a sheath-knife, sandpapered by hand and treated with cooking oil.

Goblets and cups

To drink out of a wooden drinking vessel is an unusual experience and one well worth having. The people of

These punch cups are made from birch and the mats they stand on from rot-damaged mountain ash.

northern Sweden are lucky in this respect since the making of these items is a traditional art there, where they are carved out from outgrowing lumps of twisted mountain birches and used for drinking water, coffee and other of life's good beverages! To drink out of plastic mugs, a china cup or even the finest champagne glass in no way compares with the sensation of drinking from wood. Personally, I find that these other materials interfere with the process of drinking, perhaps by absorbing part of the taste, but with wood its smoothness and texture enhance the drink allowing all the aromatic elements of the timber to merge into the taste, be it of water, milk, beer, wine or spirits.

The goblets for wine and beer together with the cups for punch shown on page 57 are of birch, a suitable damp-resisting wood. The goblets are 200mm ($7\frac{7}{8}$in) high with a diameter of 75mm (3in), and the cups are 80mm ($3\frac{1}{8}$in) high with a diameter of 70mm ($2\frac{3}{4}$in). They have been turned on a screw chuck in the same way as egg-cups. The hollowing must be done whilst your blank still has plenty of strength. Having turned it to the required cylindrical shape, hollow out the inside of the blank and sand it smooth; then shape the outside of the goblet. If the outside shaping is done before the hollowing you will almost certainly have troubles due to judder caused by the flexing of the stem.

After turning, the goblet is treated with cooking oil rubbed in by turns until you feel the wood is saturated. It should not be washed in the ordinary sense of the word and no liquid should be left in one for long. After use, rinse the goblet quickly and turn it upside down. As long as it is still new, you should oil it occasionally. Do not keep it in a warm place, rather in a cool area such as a pantry. By following this advice you should preserve your wooden drinking vessel for at least as long as your other cups and and glasses!

Wine or beer goblets turned from birch. The corkscrew and bottle stopper make up the set. Above are some suggestions for turned goblets and bowls.

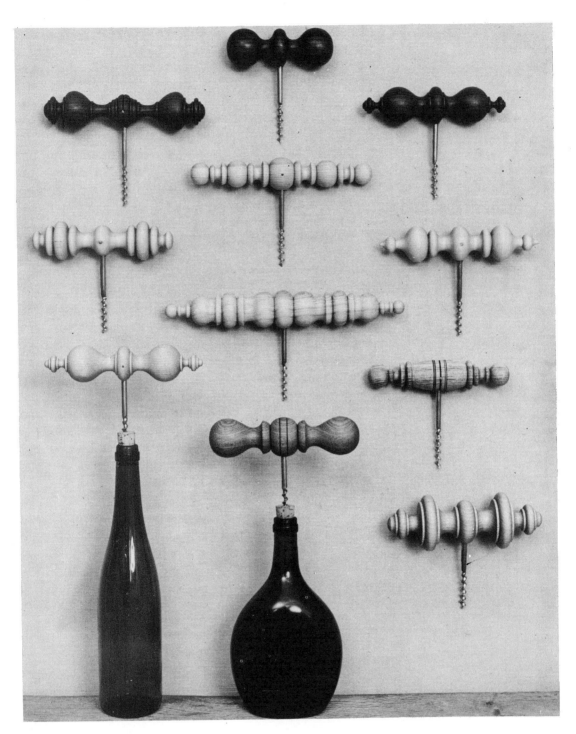

Wooden knobs galore

Stoppers for bottles

Most of us have kept empty jars and bottles at home either because they were attractive curios and seemed too nice to throw out, or in the optimistic hope that they would come in useful one day. Usually they stand about collecting dust. If, however, one can turn a pleasing knob to fix on to a cork, then the item has a new lease of life as a serving bottle or storage container. Before you start turning your stopper, study the article it is to fit and see whether you can perhaps integrate the design you produce with that of the item it will close, so creating a form of harmony.

The stoppers on pages 62 and 63 are turned from birch and old fir. The cork, which can usually be bought from any leading chemists, is attached to the turned pin of the stopper as in the diagram. A hole of corresponding diameter to the pin is drilled into the cork which is afterwards secured with waterproof, non-toxic adhesive.

The corkscrews in the picture are made from birch, old fir, oak and walnut. They have all been treated with oil.

The stoppers on the next two pages have been turned from birch and old fir. The shape of the bottle can inspire the design of the stopper.

Corkscrews

If you have made a stopper for a serving-bottle it may also be fun to turn a good corkscrew perhaps to the same

The knobs above have been made from old and new fir. The size depends on whether they are intended for cupboards or doors.

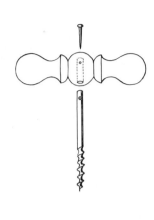

design as the stopper. It may prove difficult to get hold of the screw part, but a simple method is to buy an ordinary wooden corkscrew and take it to pieces. The screw of such items is usually attached to the handle with a pin or screw and the latter can be re-used when the new corkscrew is assembled, as shown in the diagram. When assembling your corkscrew remember to measure precisely how deep the bore hole for the screw is to be and make sure that it is accurately centred: that is the place to drill the little hole to take the securing pin. Take particular care in assembling the parts as it is easy to split the handle when pressing the screw home. The corkscrews pictured on page 60 are from 130mm ($5\frac{1}{8}$in) to 290mm ($11\frac{5}{8}$in) and made from birch, old fir, oak and walnut. They have all been treated with oil.

Wardrobe and door knobs

Wooden knobs on wardrobes, drawers and doors are pleasing to grasp and impart a rustic air which enhances the appearance of certain types of furniture. Knobs can be made in a large variety of designs according to taste and inclination. One's aim ought to be to produce an item well adjusted to the grip and aesthetically pleasing. Opposite are some examples. Size will determine whether the finished article is more suitable for a wardrobe or a drawer. The ones here are of fir between 30mm (1⅛in) and 120mm (4¾in) long and 30mm (1⅛in) to 80mm (3⅛in) wide. If you turn them on the screw chuck you will have a ready-made hole for securing them on from the back of a drawer or door. One can also turn them between centres; make a pin, drill a hole where the knob is to go and fasten it with adhesive. This method could also be adapted successfully in the making of coat pegs.

Knobs for the lavatory

The turned knob illustrated serves to show how a comparatively minor detail can make a necessary room less prosaic. The usual handle attached to the chain of the old-fashioned, high-level flushing cisterns is rather dull. The suspended handle is of birch and the others, for the more modern cistern, are of fir.

An ordinary room can be made a little less prosaic with a few turned knobs or handles. The knob suspended on the left is of birch, the others are made of fir.

Mirrors and trinkets

Wall mirrors

The mirrors illustrated here are made of fir and birch. The largest is 400mm (15$\frac{3}{4}$in) in diameter and the mirror glass 300mm (11$\frac{7}{8}$in). These mirrors have been turned in one piece including the back and the glass has been glued directly to the wood. This method presupposes your timber is dry since changes due to the drying out of a stout piece of wood can cause the glass to loosen or distort. The risk of this happening is diminished if you leave a few millimetres' gap between the edge of the glass and the rim of the frame. Usually, mirror frames are turned as a proper frame, with a rebate to take the circular mirror and wooden back, and this would, of course, reduce the problems of shrinkage in the wood. However, you will find this simple method quite satisfactory particularly for smaller mirrors. The ones here were hung by means of a leather strip, as shown in the diagram. A hole is drilled in the frame for the leather strip and a larger, shallow hole is made in the back where the ends of the strip are knotted together.

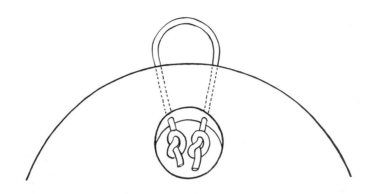

Wall mirrors made from fir and birch. The diagram above shows the method of attaching the leather thong.

Hand mirrors

Strictly speaking, hand mirrors are of the same design as the wall mirrors varying only with regard to size and the type of timber used. The dark one on page 70 is of walnut, the two others of old fir. The larger design has a glass with a diameter of 120mm (4¾in) and a frame of 175mm (6⅞in) diameter and 27mm (1¹⁄₁₆in) thickness. The handle, which is let into the frame, is 180mm (7in) long including the turned pin. The small mirror's glass has a diameter of 70mm (2¾in) and a frame of 100mm (4in), 17mm (¾in) in thickness, with a handle 115mm (4½in) long including the pin. The glass is put in place with glue in the same way as the wall mirrors.

The frames for both wall and hand mirrors can be turned in a variety of ways; those illustrated were turned on a screw chuck. Of course, a consequence of this method is that a small screw hole is left on the reverse of the mirror. However, should you wish the back to be whole and perfect, this finish can be obtained in one of two ways.

Mount the wooden disc you have chosen for your frame on a woodscrew chuck and trim the edges to a smooth circle. Mark the desired frame width on the face of the disc and hollow out the recess for the mirror glass. At this stage the worked surface should be sanded and then sealed with cellulose sealer while still on the chuck. Sand and cellulose again when dry and repeat the procedure until you have achieved the finish you want.

Remove the work from the chuck and replace with a piece of hardwood larger than your mirror frame and turn the hardwood block with a recess on the face. The recess should be of a size to accept the partially-completed mirror frame as a drive fit, with the turned face of your work going in first. In the case of the hand mirrors shown, the backs were then recessed removing the screw marks and providing a hollowed out back similar to the front. They are intended for embellishment

Hand mirrors made from walnut and old fir. The back can be turned in one piece or hollowed out and mounted with lace or embroidery.

with pillow lace or an embroidered cloth covering the back and fitted into the recess. The alternative method is described in the section on bowl turning. There the blank is glued to a softwood disc with brown paper interposed and the softwood disc screwed to the faceplate or mounted on the screw chuck.

A close-up of the mirror itself.

Pendant mirrors

Since it is often quite difficult to locate mirrors, I thought that combining their utilitarian function with a decorative one would be a good idea. If the glass itself is not felt to be a sufficiently attractive piece of jewellery, then one can merely turn the mirror back to front to display the plain, smooth back.

Pendant mirror made from pear wood which is very soft to the touch. Notice the dress-maker's dummy from the early part of the century has a turned stand.

The turning of the pendant illustrated on page 72 has been done on a screw chuck as shown in the diagram below. After mounting the blank on the chuck, turn it to a cylindrical shape. Next shape the frame of your mirror and hollow out the recess in which the mirror glass is to fit. Drill the edge of the frame to receive the dowel of the handle and smooth and finish the frame whilst it is still mounted in the lathe. Finally, when the finish is dry, part off the remaining waste from the back, which will then need sandpapering and finishing by hand. Although somewhat wasteful of timber, this method is very simple and also satisfactory for hand mirrors as well.

The mirror pictured on page 72 is of pearwood which is a very soft timber to the touch, and the finished texture can be enhanced with a rub of oil. The outer diameter is 70mm (2$\frac{3}{4}$in) and that of the glass 40mm (1$\frac{1}{2}$in). The mirror is suspended on a leather strip with a 35mm (1$\frac{3}{8}$in) fastener. Don't forget to leave a few millimetres' clearance for shrinkage and expansion between glass and wood.

Necklaces

Turning the parts of a necklace can lead to any number of creative possibilities. The one on page 74 is an example. Made from birch wood, it consists of a number of wooden beads and five parts of different length, each of the latter being turned in one piece. The longest part is 170mm (6$\frac{3}{4}$in) and the whole circumference of the necklace is roughly 1000mm (39$\frac{3}{8}$in). It is threaded on a leather thong and the ornamental part stabilised by means of a wire.

The beads are best turned up in short sticks of six or so, subsequently being parted off with a saw and finished by hand. They can, of course, be sanded in a similar way to which gem stones are polished, by placing them in a drum lined with glasspaper and attaching the drum to the faceplate of the lathe.

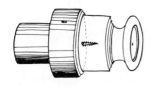

Birch necklace. The five parts of different lengths were each turned in one piece.

Lamps and furnishings

Table lamps and standard lamps

Lamps can be made to any number of different designs. Generally, they are made as individual items with little thought to integrating them with the other furniture except as regards type of wood and the design of the shade. Personally, I find my inspiration in nature, as you will have seen from the examples on pages 22 and 25. I have also been influenced by the old turnery shapes and taken suggestions from paraffin lamps, banisters and so on. The illustration on pages 78 and 79 shows lamps whose form originated from such sources. They are between 140mm (5½in) and 350mm (13¾in) high and are made of three types of timber; the dark ones are of walnut, the light ones of old or new fir and the tallest lamp the middle was turned to a different design from larch wood.

When turning lamps it is a general rule to make the base as a separate item and then mortise the upright section into it. It is often necessary to use a glued assembly to obtain a block thick enough for the body of the lamp. If you use trunk or log timber (c.f. pages 21 and 29) cracks will be as unavoidable as they are undesirable. When gluing wood to the body of the lamp, the appearance is enhanced if the annual rings can be made to form an integrated pattern (see Holders and Hat stands, page 92).

Photographed on page 77 are three standard lamps of identical design but differing in the timber used: walnut and old and new fir. They are 1100mm (43¼in) high with base diameter of 350mm (13¾in). Each has been turned in four parts, including the base. There are sound reasons for these divisions: the distance between centres your lathe will accept, the length of stock which will have to

Three standard lamps turned with the same design but made from different woods, walnut and old and new fir.

be bored to take the flex and the economical use of timber. Thus, you have natural divisions into base, lower thick turning, and the two longer sections. They are, of course, mortised together with a bead turned to conceal the joint. All the lamps have a through-hole drilled for the flex.

The standard lamp on page 80 standing amongst dried-up and moss-covered trees is 1250mm (49$\frac{1}{4}$in) high with a base diameter of 350mm (13$\frac{3}{4}$in), composed of four sections and made of new fir.

The last example on page 81 is an old-type drawing-room standard lamp in walnut. Intended to be tall and thin, it was rather difficult to make. It is 1600mm (63in) high without the shade, and the base has a diameter of 350mm (13$\frac{3}{4}$in). Due to its unusual height, I had to turn this lamp in five parts which were hard to assemble without the joints showing. The shape of the finished item is intended to give the impression of beads.

Advent candle holder

The candle holder shown on page 83 is made of fir and turned from 75mm × 75mm (3in square) wood. The base is 600mm (23$\frac{5}{8}$in) long. By sawing the piece in half lengthways one not only arrives at a rather novel form, but also produces two candle holder bases. The sockets, which are mortised into the base, have holes drilled for the usual tapers 22mm ($\frac{7}{8}$in) and 40mm (1$\frac{1}{2}$in).

Table and stools

If one looks carefully, one is sure to come across something in the home that has been turned such as the legs and back of a chair, the massive turned legs of an old table, and the ball-shaped feet of a chest or wardrobe. A more unusual example might be a bed fitted with knobs

Advent candle holder made from fir.

on top and decorations in front in the form of turned parts which are sawn off lengthwise (see page 85), a spinning-wheel, a flower pedestal or even the banisters of a staircase.

Here are examples of turned furniture in the form of a kitchen or dining table and matching stools, all made from old fir acquired from a demolition site. The table is 510mm (20in) high and the dimensions of the top are 600mm (23$\frac{5}{8}$in) × 1000mm (39$\frac{3}{8}$in). The seats are 420mm (16$\frac{1}{2}$in) high with a 380mm (15in) diameter. Notice that the turned pattern of the legs is the same for both table and stools. In this connection I should like to remind you of a point that was made earlier; the design of a single item or model can be adapted to a variety of different objects. If you compare the standard lamps on pages

Dining table and stools made from demolition timber. Notice that the turning pattern is the same although the proportions differ.

80 and 81, the spice rack on page 87, with the cups and corkscrew on page 58 you will see that a single turnery design has been enlarged or reduced to serve a variety of purposes.

The line drawings below and on page 86 illustrate respectively the end of a bed and staircase banisters, two areas which give excellent scope for turnery techniques. To turn one's own bed frame is an ambitious project about which most people only dream! How wonderful to sleep on a bed fashioned to one's own inclination; and what a practical and rewarding outcome of one's craftsmanship! If you decide to make your own you can choose between employing only one timber or several, between simple or ornate decoration, symmetry or irregularity. A satisfying piece indeed to gaze on before falling asleep!

To be able to turn a bed for himself could be a turner's dream . . .

It is in older houses that you are most likely to come across turned banisters; interestingly enough, it seems as if these are coming back into fashion. You will find much inspiration by studying them as well as the balusters of balconies and altar rails in churches. Visits to stately homes, castles and National Trust properties will give you a wealth of examples, turned over the centuries, from which to draw further ideas. Such buildings often have a considerable quantity of showy decoration both architecturally and in the furnishings. The line drawing of the staircase banister shows an older model with modern mortising; notice that the pattern of the turnery work for the balusters is the same as that of the table and stool shown on page 84.

Banisters based on an old design but with modern mortising.

Spice rack

The small spice rack illustrated below is made of old fir and has shelves 370mm (14½in) long and 100mm (4in) wide. The height, including the props, is 300mm (11¾in). The latter have been turned with a pin in each end which passes through the shelves; afterwards, knobs have been glued on to the pins which lock the shelves in place. For hanging, a small strip of wood is fitted to the upper part which takes a screw. Using this method you can produce racks with two or three props, several storeys, or even combine the design with hanging pegs to make book racks, display or hat racks.

This spice rack is made from old fir using the same turned pattern as that on page 84.

Sometimes the possession of an unusual lid can inspire you to turn a box for it. These lids came from the soot doors of old stoves and the boxes are turned from cross-grained birch with a concave bottom. Care is needed to ensure a good fit for the lid.

Practical wooden holders

Holders for paper rolls

Holders for paper rolls are useful items whether on the kitchen wall to hold paper towels for mopping up spills, on the bedside table, in the lavatory or outside as a source of napkins which the wind cannot blow away. In the photograph the small holder on the left is for toilet paper and is jocularly termed 'holder for open-air theatre tickets' in our family. This phrase originated with my maternal grandfather who, when sitting on the outside lavatory and discovering that the toilet paper had run out, would shout, 'No more tickets left!' This model, which is suitable for all standard paper sizes, could equally well be used as a stand for ring doughnuts, provided that you enlarge the base.

Turned fir holders for paper rolls of different kinds.

92

Stands for hats, caps.and wigs

Hat stands are items which used to be a common sight in the days when ladies sported large and delicate head-wear and they are still to be seen in the windows of some milliners' shops, being a perfect way of keeping a hat in shape. Nowadays they can be used as a wig stand. In the home there was often some type of hat stand and it was usual to fit the clothes rack with something of the kind. Nowadays you are most likely to see ones made of plastic or other synthetic material and only rarely the true wooden variety. The two models shown were the result of my having drawn inspiration from two original wooden hat stands. Both were turned in fir and are 500mm (19¾in) high. The shaped pieces on top have a diameter of 150mm (6in) and were made from glued-up assemblies of four pieces of wood 75mm × 75mm (3in square).

Carefully made, such a stand has an ornamental value quite apart from its usefulness. The craftsman should take particular pains when assembling the top piece. It should be a matter of course to ensure that the heart-wood faces outwards when several pieces of wood are glued together and one should try to fit the graining in such a way that the glued join becomes smooth and forms a homogeneous pattern on the top.

The diagram shows how blocks can be fitted and glued together in such a way as to produce a homogenous pattern on the top after they are turned.

Left: hat stands turned from fir show the pleasing effect of the grain.

Key tags

Apart from being a good method of differentiating between your keys, a wooden key tag is a good substitute for worry beads! The small tags illustrated on page 94 are between 70mm (2¾in) and 90mm (3½in) long and turned in an assortment of woods: old fir, walnut, birch, juniper and laburnum. The two larger tags are 170mm (6¾in) long and turned in old fir. I got the idea for making them after a recent visit to a local restaurant; wanting to use the

These key tags have been made from old fir, walnut, birch, juniper and laburnum. They are hanging on coat pegs made from old fir.

lavatory, I was alarmed to discover that I was expected to borrow a key with a plastic tag about two feet long inscribed with the word 'Toilet' in large capitals, far too big to be discreetly put in the pocket or, for that matter, to forget to return, thus heralding my destination for all to see! These wooden tags would be rather uncomfortable if left in a pocket and have the added advantage of anonymity; they are reliable, attractive and cannot be easily lost.

Implements with wooden handles

Handles for old tools

One way of giving a face-lift to tools is to turn a new handle for a worn-down rake or an old hammer. This gives you an opportunity of making handles appropriate to your own grip and to a design you want. To those of you who might wonder at the point of re-vamping, say, an old rake, let me remind you that in the past it was a general custom to decorate the implements of labour with scrolls and patterns to relieve the wearisome work. The new handles illustrated on page 97 are made of birch. The dark marks have been produced by a cut with a chisel and afterwards the edge of a piece of paper or the sharp point of a splinter is held against the cut until it gets hot. Take care, as it is easy to burn too much; after all, this is one of the earliest methods of creating fire!

These new handles turned from birch use traditional turning patterns.

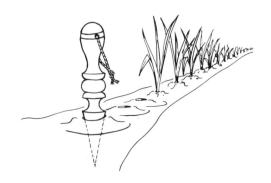

This dibber made from birch is a useful tool for planting, sowing seeds or laying bulbs.

Dibbers

Dibbers are convenient little tools for putting things into the soil, either plants or bulbs in the garden or seeds in a flower pot. Of course, however plain the shape this tool serves its purpose but is more fun with some decoration. They can be made with either a long or short handle, and in a variety of shapes and kinds of wood although it is obviously best to choose a hardy type, such as birch or oak. The dibber in the photograph is of birch, 260mm $(10\frac{1}{4}$in) long with a cone 100mm × 40mm (4in × $1\frac{1}{2}$in).

Chairman's gavel

A gavel is the medium for all sorts of important pronouncements and is most commonly connected with

Chairman's gavel made from teak. The head of the gavel needs a heavy wood such as teak, oak, beech or elm.

auctions or court rooms; it carries the weight of authority and is therefore invested with more status than its size might suggest! The gavel depicted here is teak and made in two parts. The head is 70mm × 90mm (2$\frac{3}{4}$in × 3$\frac{1}{2}$in) and the handle 40mm × 250mm (1$\frac{1}{2}$in × 9$\frac{7}{8}$in). In choosing the wood, at least for the head if not for the entire piece, take a somewhat heavy timber such as teak, oak, beech or elm. These will ensure that the gavel resounds strongly at a decision. If you have the opportunity, take a look at the gavel used at local committee meetings or a club. This would make a good presentation gift.

A woodturner's dining table

With this photograph I should like to conclude by showing you my idea of perfection: a wooden table set up in the open air under the trees and spread with dishes, platters and goblets all of wood, to partake of nature's store from objects made from nature's bounty.

A few words from the woodturner

I hope this book has been instrumental in giving the reader impetus and confidence in fostering his own ideas, showing how it is possible to take suggestions and inspiration from what is, after all, our greatest strength: nature. Besides that, it is my fond wish to keep alive the old craft of turning so that the tradition may continue into the future.

A few words of advice for those of you who intend to start work: think twice before you begin, firstly of any possible accident risk from the lathe and secondly of the method in which the material should be worked. Our forebears had comparatively simple machinery on which they managed to produce some exquisitely beautiful pieces; today we have modern lathes and a wide choice of ancillary equipment. This means that the work is a lot easier in many ways but, at the same time, the faster machines are also far more dangerous.

One way of avoiding unnecessary accidents is to wear sensible clothing; do not have large quantities of fabric hanging free, loose-fitting shirts or ties, rather select simple, lightweight items which will tear easily if they are inadvertently caught and will not drag you into the lathe. If you have long hair, be sure to tie it well back or secure it in a cap. The most important factor in the elimination

of accidents is the turner's concentration; be sure that you are well rested and alert.

In turning as opposed to other crafts such as working in clay, glass or sheet metal you must have a clear idea of the shape you are aiming for from the outset; there is no possibility of changing anything at a later stage if your medium is wood. This is a disadvantage when compared with workers in the above media who can always begin again should they feel that something has gone drastically wrong. For the turner, a mistake is definitive, for it is hardly possible to replace wood that has been cut away! If you are doing some simple turnery, there is always a possibility of exchanging the material, but if you are dealing with a unique item fashioned from a rare timber or a piece specially shaped by natural causes, failure is doubly irritating. One way of avoiding such a disaster is to ensure that the lathe speed is not too high, to begin with a low speed so that the material can revolve freely before you start the motor (particularly if the shape to be turned is irregular) and to use tools appropriate to the job and well sharpened.

Finishing

Providing that the article you have made is not to be used for edibles, linseed oil gives a very good finish, albeit that it involves a considerable amount of work. However, the resulting finish which enhances the beauty of the wood is well worth the effort.

Use boiled linseed with five per cent white spirit to five per cent terebine. The mixture may be warmed before use but this is not essential. The oil should be rubbed in well and then off so that only the thinnest possible coating remains. Each coat must be allowed to cure before the next is applied; normally it will harden overnight. Cover each time with brown paper to keep off dust. The oil hardens by contact with air and if sealed in too early with another coat will never harden. On normal hardwoods twenty such coats will produce an excellent finish.

Woodturning is a pleasant and stimulating craft and one that need be neither complicated nor expensive. Fundamentally it is very simple; a power makes the material spin and there is some form of arrangement to hold it in place while work is in progress. In the dim and distant past our ancestors placed the material to be turned between their feet and some appropriate hold. For a driving force they had a form of string, a leather strip or a tough cord which was wound round the article to be turned. With one hand they pulled the string up and down, making the article spin, and with the other did the 'turning' by means of a sharp tool.

Last I should like to thank all those who have made it possible for me to write this book, especially my wife Britt Marie who has helped me and given her support, and my good friend Johnny who has acted as photographer and collaborated with me. My thanks, too, to all those who have previously bought articles from me and have kindly loaned them for photographing within the text.

Bibliography

Bibliography

Other Books on Woodturning

ENSINGER, EARL W. *Problems in Artistic Woodturning.* Woodcraft Supply, 1978.

GUSTAVSON, RAGNER, AND OLLIE OLSON. *Creating in Wood with the Lathe.* New York: Van Nostrand Reinhold, 1968.

HOLTZAPFFEL, JOHN J. *The Principles and Practice of Hand or Simple Turning,* reprint of 1881 edition. New York: Dover, 1976.

———. *The Principles and Practice of Ornamental or Complex Turning,* reprint of 1894 edition. New York: Dover, 1973.

PETERS, GEOFF. *Woodturning.* New York: Arc Books, 1962.

STOKES, GORDON. *Beginner's Guide to Woodturning.* Levittown, N.Y.: Transatlantic Arts, 1975.

———. *Woodturning for Pleasure.* Englewood Cliffs, N.J.: Prentice-Hall, 1980.

Arts and Crafts Books from Spectrum

BAKKE, KAREN, *The Sewing Machine as a Creative Tool.*(New opportunities to be creative with a sewing machine: applique, patchwork, drawing, quilting, and other techniques.

BELFER, NANCY, *Designing in Batik and Tie Dye.* Step-by-step directions for tie dye; explains uses for different types of fabric, dyes, waxes, and bindings.

———— , *Designing in Stitching and Applique.* How to use readily available material to create beautiful stitching and applique works.

BERLYE, MILTON K., *How to Sell Your Artwork: A Complete Guide for Commercial and Fine Artists.* How to successfully sell paintings, prints, sculpture, and all types of commercial art.

CHRISTENSEN, JO IPPOLITO, *The Needlepoint Book: 303 Stitches with Patterns and Projects.* Basic techniques of designing, doing, and finishing needlepoint works.

_____ , *Needlepoint: The Third Dimension.* How to use and combine stitches to create new works; directions for working the design and background in one direction, transferring original designs onto canvas, stitching left-handed, and much more.

_____ , *Teach Yourself Needlepoint.* Over fifty needlepoint projects divided into different skill levels, with tips on every aspect of the craft from supplies and procedures to the use of color and design.

COLLETTI, JACK J., *The Art of Woodcarving.* Simple instructions to show readers how to develop and perfect carving skills.

CONRAD, JOHN W., *The Ceramics Manual.* Comprehensive introduction for the beginner and an invaluable reference guide for the experienced in ceramics.

DERKATSCH, INESSA, *Transparent Watercolor: Painting Methods and Materials.* Instructions for everything from selecting good quality brushes to avoiding common watercolor problems.

DiPASQUALE, DOMINIC, JEAN DELIUS, AND THOMAS ECKERSLEY, *Jewelry Making: An Illustrated Guide to Technique.* Introduction to every aspect of hand-crafted jewelry.

DONAHUE, BUD, *The Language of Layout.* Practical information and techniques used by the professional artist.

FOSS, MILDRED, *Creative Embroidery with Your Sewing Machine.* How to use a sewing machine to create a wide variety of beautiful designs.

HILL, EDWARD, *The Language of Drawing.* Drawing as a "visual language" and its main components, such as expression and form.

HOWELL-KOEHLER, NANCY, *Soft Jewelry: Design, Techniques, Materials*. Guide to creating personalized jewelry in needlepoint, leather molding, macrame, and other craft techniques.

HOWER, VIRGINIA, *Weaving, Spinning, and Dyeing: A Beginner's Manual*. Self-instructional book on fundamental techniques of hand weaving.

INGHAM, ROSEMARY, AND LIZ COVEY, *The Costumer's Handbook*. Complete guide to designing and constructing stage costumes that are both practical and historically accurate.

JAMES, MICHAEL, *The Quiltmaker's Handbook*. Complete instructional manual illustrating each stage of the quiltmaking process.

JENKINS, PEGGY DAVISON, *Art for the Fun of It*. The philosophy of art education and its many benefits to children: almost every medium including drawing, painting, carving, printing, and more.

———— , *The Magic of Puppetry*. How making and playing with puppets can help children develop better communication skills, express their creativity, and release repressed emotions; instructions for over thirty types of puppets.

LEVENSON, HELENE, *Creating an Interior*. Planning and creating comfortable and attractive interiors; scores of ideas for modifying or creating a new and unique decor.

LIPPMANN, GIDON, AND DOROTHY ERSKINE, *Sew It Yourself: How to Make Your Own Fashion Classics*. Techniques needed to master the art of creating clothing.

MAXWELL, WILLIAM C., *Printmaking: A Beginning Handbook. Complete guide to the various aspects of printmaking.*

MILANI, LUCILLE, *Tailoring the Easy Way.* How to get professional looking results in sewing clothing for both women and men.

MYERS, STANLEY, A.I.A., AND RICHARD FIGIEL, *Creative Home Remodeling.* A working alternative to the high cost of new housing: complete process of remodeling, from planning the house design to installing security systems in the home.

NASH, GEORGE, *Old Houses: A Rebuilder's Manual.* A practical road map to recovering and preserving the spirit of an old house while making structural and cosmetic repairs.

PECOR, CHARLES J., *The Craft of Magic: Easy-to-Learn Illusions for Spectacular Performances.* The techniques and the psychology of illusions; step-by-step illustrated instructions.

PROVENZO, EUGENE F., AND ASTERIE BAKER PROVENZO, *The Historian's Toybox: Children's Toys from the Past You Can Make Yourself.* Guide to making historical toys, with scores of anecdotes and simple instructions.

QUIRKE, LILLIAN, *The Rug Book: How to Make all Kinds of Rugs.* Demonstrates rug painting, crocheting, weaving, knitting, and needlepoint techniques for making rugs.

RICHARDSON, JOHN ADKINS, *The Complete Book of Cartooning.* Guide to drawing all types of cartoons and caricatures and to getting them published.

ROSENBERG, SHARON, AND JOAN WEINER BORDOW, *The Denim Book.* How to recycle denim; techniques and directions for making pants, skirts, tops, and accessories.

RUTAN, JACKIE, *The Perfect Fit: Easy Pattern Alterations.* How to pick patterns, redesign patterns to fit perfectly, cut and sew fabrics, and design original clothing from commercial patterns.

SIMMONS, SEYMOUR, III, AND MARC S. A. WINER, *Drawing: The Creative Process*. All phases of drawing from landscape and still-life to portraits and animal drawing: the mechanics of drawing as well as the creative act of seeing as the basis for creative expression.

SMITH, EDWARD, *Gemcutting: A Lapidary Handbook*. Illustrated guide to the art of gemcutting; simple directions for everything from grinding, sanding, and polishing.

TERMINI, MARIA, *Silkscreening*. Illustrated guide to the techniques, procedures, and supplies of silkscreening.

TIMMONS, VIRGINIA G., *Designing and Making Mosaics*. Every step in the creation of mosaics, from designing to finishing and framing the work.

TONEY, ANTHONY, *Painting and Drawing: Discovering Your Own Visual Language*. Progress from drawing simple lines to complex contour drawing and painting with easy-to-follow exercises.

VISHER, M.A., *The Finishing Touch: Restore, Repair, and Refinish Your Furniture*. Guide to repairing scratches, gouges, blistering veneer, and other blemishes that may mar the beauty of furniture.

WETTLAUFER, GEORGE AND NANCY, *The Craftsman's Survival Manual*. How to make a full or part-time living at any craft.

Index

K
Key tags, 93, 95
Knives, 57
Knobs, 65-66
Knots, 23

L
Laburnum, 43, 46, 93
Ladder, 51
Lantern 26, 27
Lamp stand, 23, 28, 41
Larch, 76
Lavatory handle, 66
Linseed oil, 19, 29, 41, 104

M
Mirrors, 68-75
Mountain ash, 41, 42, 43

N
Necklaces, 75

O
Oak:
    candle holder, 17
    corkscrew, 65
    cutting board, 55
    dibber, 99
    gavel, 101
Offcuts, 46
Oil finish, 46, 65, 75
    Olive, 54, 55, 56, 59
    proprietary, 55
Olive oil, 54, 55, 56, 59